Pat & Joe —

Thank you for com[illegible] :)
magnificent corner of the [illegible] feel
memories of vistas, lakes, fishing, hiking,
eating, drinking, celebrating friendship —
and the Tetons!! Lots of love Kathy —

July 12, 2008

Glad you came!

LOCAL COLOR

Jackson Hole in Words & Watercolor

Huntley Baldwin

HUNTLEY BALDWIN

WHITE WILLOW PUBLISHING

White Willow Publishing
Box 6464
Jackson, Wyoming 83002
whitewillow@bresnan.net

ISBN   0-9755359-1-9
EAN   978-0-9755359-1-2
Printed in China

"I don't mind hiking, but I'd rather walk in the city where there's more to see."

—Dana Baldwin, Age 17

Autumn, Oxbow Bend

SUMMER

AUTUMN

MUD SEASON
(NOT PICTURED)

CONTENTS

Disclaimers, Explanations & Acknowledgments

First, let's clarify "local." Jackson Hole oldtimers will tell you you're not really a local unless you were born and raised here. No one who arrived after The Gap opened counts. I confess that I was born in a city (Washington, D.C.) and worked in a city (Chicago). But we've lived here, winters included, for 11 years now, after many years of visits. Jackson Hole is home. So I donned the mantle of "local" and set out to share insider secrets of the pleasures of life in Jackson Hole with those less fortunate.

Second, unlike virtually every other local, be they oldtimer or newcomer, I don't ski. Except for snowshoeing and cross-country skiing I mostly stay indoors and paint during ski season. This explains why summer and fall activities receive more attention in this book. We also try to sneak out of town in May until the last of the snow melts and summer takes hold. This explains why "spring," the elusive fourth season, receives no attention.

Third, not every painting was done in plein air, as one might expect of a journal or sketchbook. Many were done in the studio based on photos I took in plein air. This explains why some are tidier than others.

Finally, the book is not overly serious. It is, I hope, accurate and useful. Generally, I've tried to be "serious" with the paintings but playful with the text. From the outset this book has had trouble deciding exactly what it wanted to be. Part journal, part guidebook, part sketchbook, part commentary, it ended up with a little something for everyone. For someone who has never been to Jackson Hole it serves as invitation and incentive; for the new visitor it contains practical tips on things to see and do; for the frequent visitor it is a scrapbook of memories; and for other "locals" it is simply another reminder of why we live in this very special place.

Several people deserve special thanks: wildlife photographer Franz Camenzind for photo reference for some of the animal pictures; watercolorist and teacher Fred Kingwill for helping an oil painter through the frustrations of a new medium; my publisher, editor and muse Becky Woods Bloom for helping to turn pages of paintings into an actual book; and most of all, my wife Joan, who happily and willingly agreed to leave one life and move to Jackson Hole and begin another.

When we first drove into Jackson Hole to stay it was June. White-capped mountains jutting from a green valley. Bright sunlight and clear blue skies. Two days later, when the moving van arrived, it

GREEN
(summer)

snowed. Although it is the unofficial start of summer, June can go either way. Warm and sunny ideally, the dominant green dotted with colorful wildflowers. If it is cold and rainy you just tell yourself it's a good forest fire deterrent. In early summer fishermen must still wait for the Snake to clear and backpackers must still contend with snow-packed trails in higher elevations. But rafters and kayakers never complain about a high, fast river and there are plenty of dry trails in the valley. By July the Grand Teton Music Festival is up and running, complementing a full array of outdoor activities: hiking, biking, boating, fishing, camping, horseback riding, scenic and whitewater rafting. Days are long and nights are cool. Okay, we get some mosquitoes. Nothing's perfect. And what starts out moist and green gradually dries and browns. But summer is the season everyone in Jackson Hole waits for. Enjoy it while it lasts.

"You have such a big sky!"

A friend visiting from a valley in the Austrian alps made this observation as she looked out over Jackson Hole.

11

Meet the neighbors

One of the nice things about living in Jackson Hole is that you don't have to venture far from home to observe wildlife. In addition to all the usual suspects -- squirrels and chipmunks, ravens and songbirds -- our yard has been visited frequently by great gray owls, moose and mule deer and on occasion by elk, ermines, coyotes, a porcupine, snowshoe hares, a pine marten and a young black bear. Most residents have a similar list. Some could even add a lynx, mountain lion and wolf.

Arrowleaf Balsamroot. Mules Ear and Arnica make yellow the first predominant wildflower color of early summer.

16

4 COMMON VARIETIES

LUPINE

Columbine

Indian Paintbrush with Aspen

Beauty...

SCARLET GILIA

FIREWEED

LITTLE WHITE FLOWERS

WILDFLOWERS

Wildflowers, for me, are like people I meet at a cocktail party. I enjoy them at the time, but when I see them again a year later I don't always remember their names. In my defense, over 600 species of Lupine have been identified.

Coneflower

... She loves me not.
Proving that looks aren't everything, the Oxeye Daisy is high on Weed & Pest Control's hit list.

...and the beast

A WALK AROUND JENNY LAKE

And other short hikes in the Park

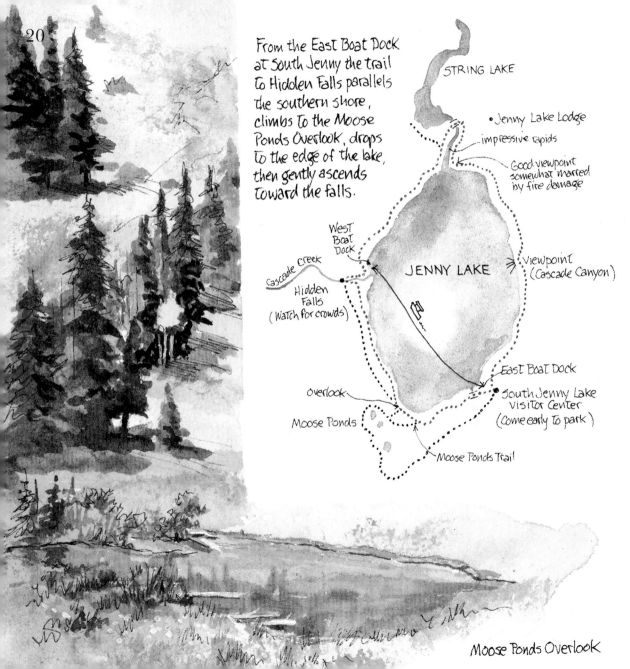

From the East Boat Dock at South Jenny the trail to Hidden Falls parallels the southern shore, climbs to the Moose Ponds Overlook, drops to the edge of the lake, then gently ascends toward the falls.

STRING LAKE

• Jenny Lake Lodge

impressive rapids

Good viewpoint somewhat marred by fire damage

West Boat Dock

Cascade Creek

Hidden Falls (Watch for crowds)

JENNY LAKE

Viewpoint (Cascade Canyon)

East Boat Dock

South Jenny Lake Visitor Center (Come early to park)

Overlook

Moose Ponds

Moose Ponds Trail

Moose Ponds Overlook

When you begin
to hear the roar of
cascading water
you'll also hear
the voices of the
tourists coming
up from the boat
dock.

Hidden Falls

From the West Boat Dock below Hidden Falls, the trail continues along the northwest shore to a footbridge spanning String Lake Outlet where a postcard view of the mountains has been somewhat marred by a recent forest fire. Cross the bridge and turn right onto the trail to continue around the east side of the lake. You'll pass a popular scenic overlook opposite Cascade Canyon on the way back to your starting point at the South Jenny parking area.

SHORT CUT. Shuttle boat across Jenny Lake.

Red berries, blue water along Jenny Lake

Jenny Lake
near the
String Lake
Outlet.
Visible evidence
of the 1999
Alder Fire.

23

String Lake

LEIGH LAKE

To Paintbrush Canyon

0.8 mi

steep uphill

0.8 mi

1.3 miles Good views

PICNIC AREA

STRING LAKE

JENNY LAKE LODGE

0.3 mi

To South Jenny Lake

FIRE DAMAGE

FIRE DAMAGE
To Hidden Falls

JENNY LAKE

The String Lake picnic area where you can begin this pleasant 3.3 mile loop is very popular (read crowded), as is the easy, flat portion of trail toward Leigh Lake. The crowds thin on the mountain side as the trail climbs through forest and wildflowers, providing nice views of the lake. The trail around String Lake intersects the trail to Paintbrush Canyon, so you may encounter serious backpackers.

A walk along Leigh Lake
Destination: Bearpaw Lake

The Leigh Lake trailhead is at the north end of the String Lake parking lot. After about .9 mile the trail divides. Follow the canoe portage trail to the right. The path along the lake is wide and level with fine views of the mountains across the lake and frequent spots for a lakeside picnic. From the divide it's 2.8 miles to Bearpaw Lake but you can turn back anytime and have had a satisfying hike.

GRANITE CANYON

A favorite hike, especially early in the summer when Granite Creek, which the trail follows, is swollen with run-off. From the trailhead at the southern end of the Moose-Wilson Road the trail passes through a sagebrush meadow, crosses Granite Creek and joins the Valley Trail. Shortly after recrossing the creek the canyon trail turns left and the uphill hiking begins. Hike as far as you wish. You'll be treated to many views of the cascading creek.

As beautiful as the canyon is, it was misnamed. The predominant rocks are gneiss, not granite.

PHELPS LAKE

At the end of a bumpy two-mile road off the Moose-Wilson Road is the Death Canyon Trailhead, starting point for numerous rigorous hikes and this pleasantly easy one. Phelps Lake Overlook is reached in just under a mile, by a trail that meanders gradually uphill through forest and wildflowers.

To Death Canyon

.9 mi

To Taggart

Phelps Lake Overlook

.7 mi

Death Canyon Trailhead

Steep Switchbacks

To Moose-Wilson Road

PHELPS LAKE

Valley Trail to Granite Canyon

BRADLEY AND BEYOND
A one-way, two-car, two-lake hike

Leave one car at the Lupine Meadows trailhead and return to the Taggart Parking area. Follow the Taggart-Bradley trail, then Bradley when the trail splits. After an uphill, downhill hike through the trees you'll reach the shore of Bradley Lake (elev. 7022 ft).

Trail up to Amphitheater Lake

Downhill, sometimes along spine of ridge with views on both sides

1.7 miles

relatively level stretch

Steady uphill climb with good lake views

1.4 miles

BRADLEY LAKE

Footbridge

Trail back to Taggart Lake

Roller coaster hills through tall conifer

Good views of Taggart Lake

0.9 miles

easy uphill

TAGGART LAKE

Taggart Lake Trail

1.3 mil

Taggart Lake from the Bradley Lake Trail

The trail climbs the moraine above Bradley, then descends through forest to Lupine Meadows.

LUPINE MEADOWS
PARKING AREA

easy level finish

TAGGART CREEK
PARKING AREA

Bradley Lake

Signal Mountain

The Signal Mountain Road is the lazy man's alternative to a 5.5 mile roundtrip hike to the summit for a spectacular view of Jackson Hole. A good spot to pickup the hiking trail is beside a pond a mile up the road. The trail gains only 633 feet to the overlook but most of it occurs in the final mile. The area is considered a good place to see wild-life and includes some berry patches popular with bears, which for many is another argument in favor of making the trip by car.

JACKSON LAKE

Dam

SNAKE RIVER

Signal Mt. Lodge

Signal Mountain Road

SIGNAL MT.

Moose Pond

TRAIL

PARK ROAD

Regardless of whether you hike or drive, consider rewarding yourself with a stop at the lakeside Signal Mountain Lodge for their justly famous nachos.

34

A hike you can drive to!

Chapel of the Transfiguration

Chapel and Cathedral (Group)

Museum with a view

If you get frustrated trying to see wildlife by driving around the Valley, stop in the National Museum of Wildlife Art. Tucked discreetly into a hillside overlooking the Elk Refuge, the museum has an impressive collection of wildlife paintings and sculpture and the building itself is worth a look (as is the view from the parking lot).

On your mark...

GAMES CHISELERS PLAY

Chiselers, a.k.a. Uinta Ground Squirrels, like to hide in the grass at the edge of roads until they see a car coming. Then, at the last possible second, they make a dash trying to reach the other side before the car reaches them.

Some win, some lose.

Unfortunately, larger mammals like moose, deer and elk play a similar game, so drive carefully.

Elk

The Elk Refuge Road

Crowded with gawkers and photographers the year a mountain lion took up residence in the rocks beside the road, this is usually a quiet stretch to walk, jog or bike.

43

Bird watching from the highway

Trumpeter Swan

Osprey
(Gone fishin')

A family of ospreys presides over
an ever changing population of
birds in the wetlands
between Highway 22
and Puzzleface Ranch.

Sandhill
Crane

Canada Goose

SKI LAKE

This 6-mile round trip hike is rated "moderate" by the Forest Service sign. It starts at the Phillips Canyon Trailhead on Teton Pass and climbs 1000 feet to a small lake. The first stretch wends uphill across a south-facing slope that can be resplendent with wildflowers.

ENGELMANN SPRUCE

There's a short, shady, level stretch through tall spruce trees before the trail drops to a marshy meadow and intersects a trail to Phillips Canyon. The trail to Ski Lake climbs for another mile.

There are broad vistas on this steep stretch. I enjoy them more on the downhill return.

STICKY GERANIUM

The last leg

The agony

and the ecstasy.   Snow King Mt.

Before you decide to move to Jackson Hole you should know this: some people who live here walk up and down Snow King FOR FUN. "The Town Hill" is handy and there are spectacular views of the Valley, but it is a walk to test legs and lungs. Just about a mile but a gain of 1000 vertical feet, Snow King is a relentlessly steep hike. At the top there's a little self-guided nature walk. If you want to save your thighs to walk another day you can ride the chair lift down. You can ride the lift up, too. But you don't get to brag about that.

Ye Olde Pass

Just over a mile up Hwy 22 from the Stagecoach Bar, Trail Creek Rd. branches off to the left and about a half mile later deadends at a parking area that is the trailhead for a hiking, biking and dog walking road to the top of Teton Pass. The Old Pass Road lies below the highway that replaced it.

If you don't want to climb to the top, there's an easy half-walk, half-hike loop.

Balsamroot and sticky geraniums border the road, plants poke through the old paving

Road

Follow the old paved road to a Tiny lake. Just beyond the lake you'll see a dirt road on the left that goes under power lines and becomes a foot path that goes through the trees, crosses Trail Creek (a wet crossing in early summer) and rejoins the road just above the parking area.

Crater Lake.
A nice destination for a short loop hike.

51

Two popular dog walks (and winter cross-country ski tours) start at the Wilson Bridge. One from the northeast parking area travels north along the east bank of the Snake toward views of the Tetons.

The other heads south along the west bank. In the summer, the west bank on both sides of the bridge is busy with rafts and fishing boats leaving and arriving and "beach activities." In addition to guaranteed dog sightings, you may also see moose munching willows by the river.

A: "SNAKE RIVER DIKES"
Q: "Where can I go to see a Labrador Retriever?"

WILSON

Cultural hub of the West Bank, Wilson sits at the base of Teton Pass, its air often filled with the aroma of burning brakes. At Hungry Jack's General Store you can buy a quart of milk, a pair of blue jeans.

"Uncle Nick"

rent a movie and pickup a copy of the New York Times. A citizen-sponsored Green Knoll Memorial commemorates firefighters who battled a 2001 forest fire. No home or firefighter was lost.

Wilson Wetlands Trail

TWO LOCAL TRADITIONS

BREAKFAST AT NORA'S. Bill Clinton ate here when he was President, but on a regular basis it's mostly regulars. SUNDAY NIGHT AT THE 'COACH You'll see silver belt buckles from the rodeo and Rodeo Drive. Drink beer, shoot pool and dance to the Stagecoach Band.

A drive up the Gros Ventre

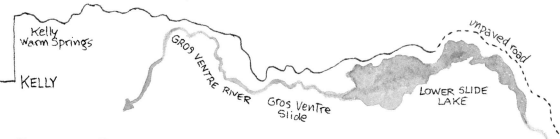

Kelly Warm Springs

KELLY

GROS VENTRE RIVER

Gros Ventre Slide

LOWER SLIDE LAKE

unpaved road

RED HILLS

To venture off the beaten path, take the Gros Ventre Road as it follows the river of the same name into red rock country. You'll often see bison on the flats between the highway and Kelly.

Teton view from the Gros Ventre Road just above the Gros Ventre River Ranch

Past Kelly Warm Springs the road climbs through aspens and emerges to overlook the river before descending to a dude ranch. It then climbs again for more spectacular views.

At Lower Slide Lake the road gets a bit more challenging, but the striking combination of red cliffs and green ranch lands is worth minor vehicle abuse.

Bring a picnic lunch and your fly rod.

LOWER SLIDE LAKE

Canoeing on String Lake and beyond

String Lake is the most user-friendly lake in the park, very popular for family boating. It's very shallow and the water is warm enough for swimming without risking hypothermia.

For the more adventurous there is a short portage to Leigh Lake. Bigger, deeper and colder, Leigh Lake can be threatening when afternoon winds come up. Campsites across the lake are popular with overnight campers and bears.

Mergansers

Fly fishermen

FLOATING THE SNAKE

A Sundowner Picnic

There aren't many places in Jackson Hole that don't offer a beautiful view but few are more sweeping than the view from Curtis Canyon Overlook. From this knoll you look across the Elk Refuge with Town to the south and the Tetons to the north.

We like to pack a picnic supper and go up in the evening in time to watch the sun go down behind the mountains.

VIEW FROM CURTIS CANYON OVERLOOK

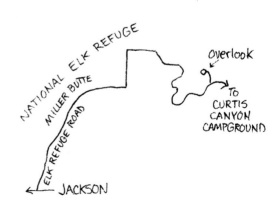

GOLD
(autumn)

As Labor Day approaches change is in the air. The days get shorter, the air gets cooler. Empty hook-ups appear between previously wall-to-wall RVs. Chiselers no longer cheat death with mad scampers across the highway. You can find a place to park downtown. "No Vacancy" signs in motels are disappearing and "Help Wanted" ads are appearing as visitors and summer workers head for home before the snow flies. Fall, a notoriously short season, is coming to Jackson Hole. September and October are our best-kept secrets, a time when locals reclaim their valley for two of its most glorious months. If we're lucky, fall is an extension of summer, with color. Or it can be a preview of winter with early cold and snow. Aspens and cottonwoods turn color, imbuing the creeks and rivers with a golden glow in time for some of the best fishing of the year. The eerie squeals of bugling elk fill the crisp evening air.

And did I mention you can find a parking place?

AUTUMN ASPENS
One reason not to leave Jackson Hole in the fall

Not the multi-colors of autumn in Vermont, but enough to warm the spirit and prepare it for the long winter months just around the corner.

OXBOW BEND   A good place to see moose (Bring binoculars.)

WOLVES

"And the lion shall lie down with the lamb but the lamb won't get much sleep."
— Woody Allen

That wolf-like creature you see loping across the Elk Refuge may be one of the new arrivals. More likely it will be one of their smaller cousins, the coyote.

Local sheep and cattle aren't the only ones made uneasy by the reintroduction of wolves into Yellowstone in 1995-96. Elk have some reason for concern. While ranchers and hunters debate conservationists over future wolf management plans, wolf watching continues to be a popular pasttime in the Jackson Hole area. There are several organized trips to Yellowstone to see the wolves or, with luck, you might see one around here.

I am not a wolf.

Some years ago, a man cited for shooting one of the protected wolves offered a rather disquieting defense: "I thought it was a dog."

Coyote

69

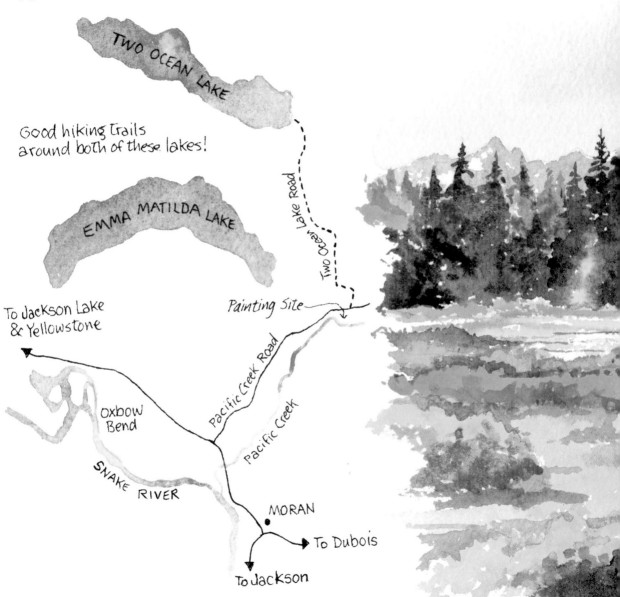

TWO OCEAN LAKE

Good hiking trails
around both of these lakes!

EMMA MATILDA LAKE

Two Ocean Lake Road

Painting Site

To Jackson Lake
& Yellowstone

Pacific Creek Road

Oxbow
Bend

Pacific Creek

SNAKE RIVER

MORAN

To Dubois

To Jackson

Fall Open-Air Concert

Our favorite place to enjoy the annual elk bugling is the old White Grass Ranch on the Death Canyon Road. We pack a picnic and arrive at dusk to wait for the elk to emerge from the trees that line the meadow. "Bugle" may not be the best word to describe the strained squeal the courting bull elk emit, but it is a thrilling sound. Other good concert sites: Lupine Meadows and the meadow behind Jenny Lake Lodge.

White Grass Ranch
Performances nightly during the rut

The Sleeping Indian,

a.k.a. Sheep Mountain in the Gros Ventre Range. It is easier to "see" the outline of a reclining Indian chief with his feather headdress than it is to spot any of the Big Horn Sheep that give the mountain its official name.

Big Horn Sheep

Flat Creek Ranch Getaway

Nestled at the base of the Sleeping Indian and protected by one of the worst roads you'll ever drive, Flat Creek Ranch has a colorful past. It was to this mountain hideaway that rustler/cowboy Cal Carrington brought "Cissy" Patterson, granddaughter of Chicago Tribune founder Joseph Medill, in the summer of 1917.

→

At the "Breakfast Hole"

The rest, as they say, is history and the current owners (he's Cissy's great nephew) like to share the details with guests over dinner at the lodge.

All the cabins have been lovingly restored and the setting is wild and beautiful. A visit combines luxury and comfort with a wide range of outdoor activities, most notably hiking (summit the Sleeping Indian if you wish), horseback riding and fly-fishing.

They'll even meet you part way so you don't have to drive the final five miles of the road.

Snake River Cutthroat Trout

VS.

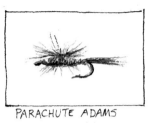

PARACHUTE ADAMS

STIMULATOR

TARANTULA

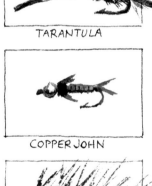

COPPER JOHN

WOOLY BUGGER

If you were going to fish Jackson Hole all season and could only use five flies, what would they be?

I put this question to local anglers and fishing guides and these were the winners.

Parachute Adams was the top vote-getter. Others varied within categories. Stimulators vied with caddis. Some preferred foam patterns or grasshoppers over the Tarantula. Everyone included a nymph and a streamer. My favorite response was, "I'd take five sizes of Parachute Adams."

TOP TEN SECRET
HOT SPOTS REVEALED
BY *LOCAL ANGLERS*

10
9
8
7
6
5
4
3
2
1

81

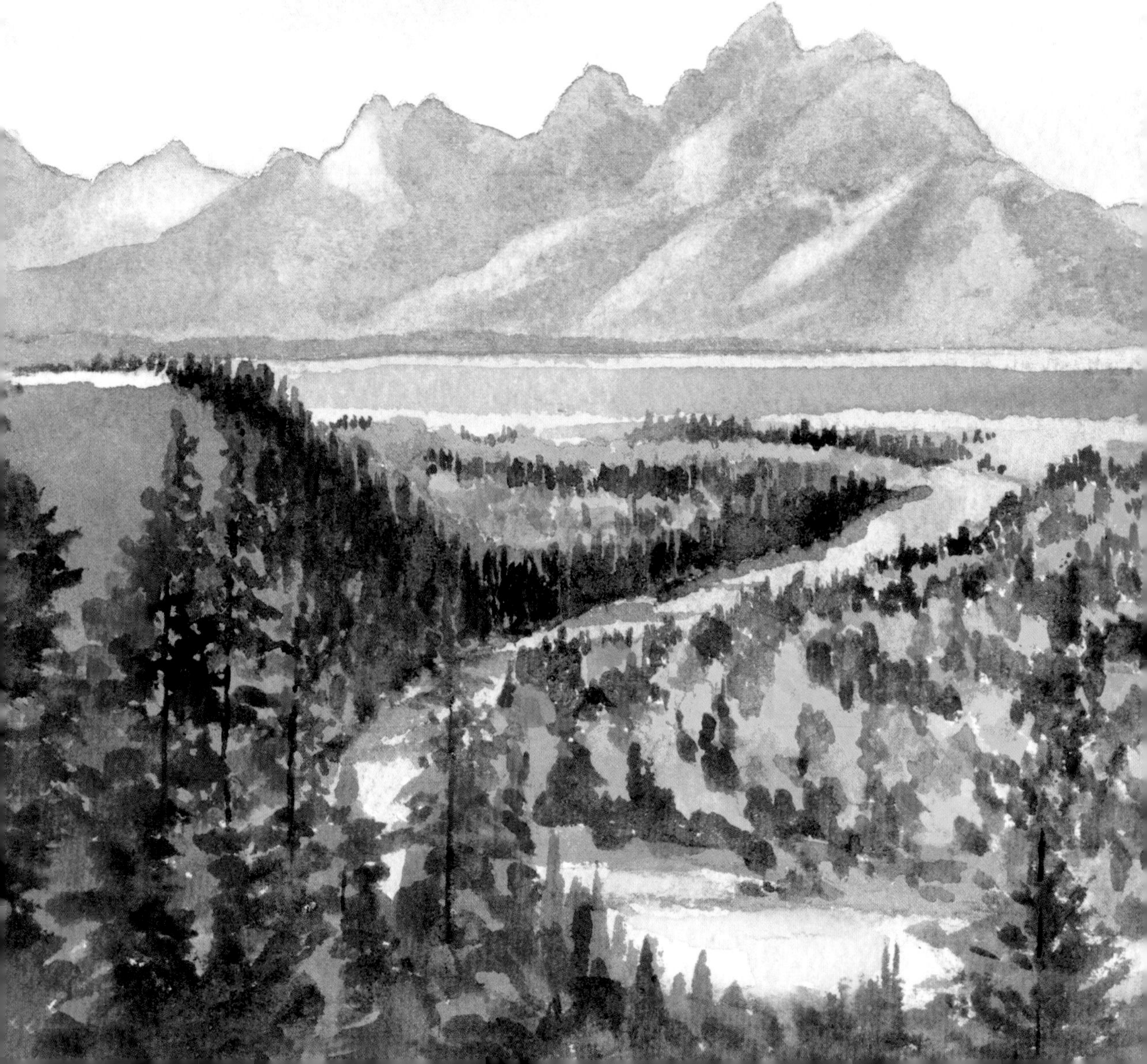

SNAKE RIVER OVERLOOK

Photographer Ansel Adams inspired countless others to snap this dramatic view of mountains and river. The turnoff is about nine miles north of Moose.

Antelope Flats Road

If you're lucky you may even
see a Pronghorn Antelope.

Bison, wildflowers and the photogenic Moulton Barn
highlight this short loop drive that circles Blacktail
Butte. The southern end begins at Gros Ventre
Junction. Drive east to the small town of Kelly, then
north to Antelope Flats Road. It rejoins the highway
just north of Moose.

The Moose~Wilson Road

This narrow, scenic road connects the Moose park entrance with the south Park entrance and Teton Village. It winds along the base of the mountains, passes ponds and marshes and is a popular wildlife viewing drive. I drove it one afternoon behind a car with out-of-state plates and a family member at every window. As they crept along, eyes peeled, looking right and left, a black bear ambled across the road behind their car. They never saw it. Timing is everything.

Coffee brewing
Simpson Lake camp

Simpson Lake. A Pack Trip.
Or, They don't call 'em The Winds for nothing.

Patches of fresh snow on the pass and serious clouds driven by stiff winds lurked in the backs of the minds of the riders gathering at the trailhead west of Dubois. After cramming too much gear into too small duffles we set out on horseback for the four hour ride to our Simpson Lake camp site, home away from home for the next six days.

Simpson Lake

Camp Life

The first night tested the limits of our good-to-20° sleeping bags but we survived and awoke to a cloudless blue sky. The sun didn't reach camp from behind the mountain until after 8:30 The sun helped but the wind was unrelenting. Monday was designated a quiet day, the only activity a short walk back down the lake to a cluster of deserted cabins. Some of us hurled beadheads into the wind but the fish were wisely laying low. Most sat in the sun and read. Monday night was even colder and the ground was crunchy with frost in the morning. After breakfast of pancakes with fresh-picked berries it was boots and saddles for an easy hour-long ride up to Pinto Lake. The trail crossed Jakeys Fork and climbed through the pines until the trees thinned. The wind was whipping across the lake with vigor but between gusts you could cast and catch some decent sized cutbows. Another virtually cloudless day and a beautiful view looking down on Simpson Lake on the ride down. The night was warmer and the next day so mild that after the sun cleared the mountain you could get by without a sweatshirt. Thirty minute hike to Dead Horse Lake. Caught enough small brook trout to keep for a meal

Domino, with a load off, awaits

Bear patiently awaits his rider, Joan

Thursday, another in a string of brisk, cloudless days. Some ride, some hike to Soapstone Lake. Pause along the way to look a sheep-eaters' "pre-form"- fragments of a soapstone bowl. At the lake wind and an absence of insects on the water conspired to shut out the fishermen. That evening before dinner we were treated to the sight of big horn sheep walking along the crest of the mountain behind camp

Willows and Pines

The last day in camp was designated another "easy day", with no organized activity. Reading in the sun (and wind) was popular. I tried fishing Simpson Lake again and the windy conditions were familiar. Finally, an 18" cutbow (it's my journal so I say it was 18") volunteered. Two smaller brookies in the afternoon rounded out a difficult week of fishing. After dinner we watched two bull moose munching in the willows among the horses. Discussion of conservation issues around the campfire, then to bed to rest up for breaking camp and the long ride out.

And so, as the sun sets slowly in the west,

a solitary fisherman takes advantage of the evening hatch on the Snake River just below Jackson Lake Dam.

WHITE (winter)

When you've grown accustomed to White Halloween you don't waste much time dreaming of a White Christmas. You count on it. Between winter's first tentative snowfall and the opening of ski season there's an awkward transition period called off-season. Whitewater rafting companies change into snowmobile tour operators. Hungry elk come out of the mountains and onto the Refuge, bracing for the coming sleigh rides. December brings serious snow. Christmas lights adorn the elk antler arches on the Town Square. Teton Pass begins to close periodically for avalanche control. Animal tracks in the snow record the night visitors to your yard. And it gets cold. Just when you thought fall was the prettiest time of the year in Jackson Hole you wake up one morning to find a foot of fresh white powder. You needn't be a downhill skier to enjoy it. Strap on snowshoes or cross-country skis and break a trail in a quiet, pristine forest. Or, if you prefer, don a Michelin Man-like suit and climb onto a snowmobile. Someone said the reason we celebrate Christmas in December is because by March everyone's sick of snow.

Meanwhile, if you like snow there's no better place than Jackson Hole in the winter.

A long,* level**ski to Jenny Lake

Because this popular, well-tracked trail is essentially level you can look up and around you now and then. Do, because the scenery is spectacular, with the dramatic Tetons dominating the view to the west. Most of the trail crosses open meadow, but stretches pass through cottonwoods and pines along Cottonwood Creek. After lunch or a snack on the shore of Jenny Lake, retrace your tracks. The slight elevation change is in your favor on the return.

*8 miles round trip
** 200 feet elevation change over 4 miles

JENNY LAKE

COTTONWOOD CREEK

PARK ROAD (CLOSED TO CARS)

parking area
(End of plowed road)

TO MOOSE

99

Snow happens.

Here's an unofficial record of four Jackson Hole winters based on how much snow I shoveled off our deck:

2002·03		2003·04		2004·05		2005·06	
10/30	6"	11/10	6"	10/29	4½"	11/14	10"
11/9	5"	11/12	5½"	10/31	2"	11/17	2"
11/10	5"	11/14	4½"	11/26	4"	11/26	4"
12/17	8"	11/27	14	12/10	13"	11/30	6"
12/21	4"	12/13	6"	12/30	8"	12/2	13½"
12/28	7"	12/14	6"	12/31	9"	12/4	1"
12/31	7"	12/25	5"	1/1	11"	12/6	2½"
2/17	8"	12/26	7"	1/3	5"	12/19	2½"
2/23	8"	12/30	15"	1/4	3"	12/20	2"
3/4	8"	1/1	6"	1/8	13"	12/29	7"
		1/2	10"	1/9	6"	12/31	9"
		1/24	5"	1/13	6½"	1/2	4"
		1/31	5"	2/7	2½"	1/3	12"
		2/17	6"	2/14	5½"	1/4	2"
		2/27	7"	2/19	7"	1/8	7"
		3/6	6"	3/19	6½"	1/12	7"
		3/27	2"			1/15	3"
						1/18	8"
						1/21	2½"
						2/2	17"
						2/5	4

More to come(ツ)

Moulton Barn

A brief history of elk antlers

BEFORE

AFTER

Moose Tracks

Winter tracks

When you hike in the summer it can sometimes seem like you have the forest to yourself. Not so in the winter. Creatures great and small leave paths of tracks that zigzag and criss-cross through the snow, some so fresh you expect to meet them around the next turn. Squirrels, snowshoe hares and other small mammals scurry across the crust making only faint impressions. Moose sink post holes so deep they appear blue at the bottom. They are all reminders that you are not alone.

Moose

"Warming house, West Thumb"

Yellowstone winter weekend

"(it is better to) sidestep or walk down the hill rather than risk skiing out of control into a boiling pool." -- Park Handout

Ski Trail to Lone Star Geyser

Old Faithful

If you can ignore the snowmobiles, Yellowstone in winter is a peaceful, pristine place. A snowcoach operates between Flagg Ranch north of Jackson Lake Lodge and Old Faithful. From the Snow Lodge (the only winter accomodations at Old Faithful) there are numerous cross-country ski trails amidst the Park's thermal features. Elk and bison wander nearby. A favorite trail winds through the trees from Kepler Cascades to Lone Star Geyser.

A snowshoe hike to Taggart Lake

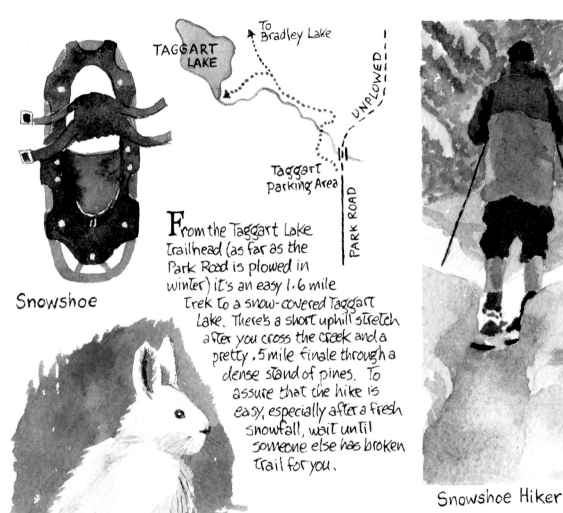

To Bradley Lake

TAGGART LAKE

UNPLOWED

Taggart Parking Area

PARK ROAD

Snowshoe

From the Taggart Lake Trailhead (as far as the Park Road is plowed in winter) it's an easy 1.6 mile trek to a snow-covered Taggart Lake. There's a short uphill stretch after you cross the creek and a pretty .5 mile finale through a dense stand of pines. To assure that the hike is easy, especially after a fresh snowfall, wait until someone else has broken trail for you.

Snowshoe Hiker

112   Snowshoe Hare

The frozen lake covered with snow, the mountain backdrop shrouded in mist, still a worthy destination.

Orange ribbon markers and the tracks of an earlier hiker made the trail easy to follow

Snake River Dikes, Revisited

This popular summer dog-walking path along the river makes a nice introduction for beginning (or cautious) cross-country skiers.

The good news is that the trail is level, easily accessible and offers clear-weather mountain views (especially along the north east Trail) with a good chance for a moose sighting in the willows.

The bad news is that it remains a popular dog walking venue and some dog owners are more conscientious than others.

APRÉS ALL

Aprés ski, aprés cross-country, aprés snowshoe, aprés anything, one of the best reasons for outdoor activity is a post-activity stop at Dornan's in Moose. Enjoy a beer or glass of wine with the Tetons literally right out the window. Besides the bar there's a grocery store, gift shop, gas station and a surprisingly well-stocked wine shop.

And should you ever want to leave Jackson Hole, Dornan's is close to the airport.

"The Village"

The vaguely European character of Teton Village's signature Tram clock Tower has been overshadowed by the growth of luxury hotel "log mahals" radiating from it. Summertime home of the Grand Teton Music Festival and year 'round home of the Mangy Moose Saloon, the Village has something for everyone. In the winter I'm told that people ski here.

JACKSON HOLE

Dornan's. A room with a view.

Jingle bells, jingle bells,

Oh what fun it is to see the elk up close from a two-horse open sleigh.

Winter on the Elk Refuge

BROWN
(postscript)

CLOSED FOR THE OFF SEASON

God holds spring out to Jackson Holers like Lucy holds a football for Charlie Brown, always snatching it away at the last minute. Warm weather is dangled tantalizingly before us only to be pulled away by yet another snowfall. Spring, a.k.a. mud season, has arrived. Too much snow for hiking, not enough for skiing. The Snake is high and muddy with runoff. The resident elk leave the Refuge as the snow recedes. Restaurants close until summer tourists replace skiers.

Spring is off-season in spades. Still, Jackson Holers make the best of the hand they're dealt. Snowmobilers have one last fling during the annual Hill Climb up Snow King Mountain. The popular "Pole-Pedal-Paddle"—a race that combines downhill and cross-country skiing, cycling and canoeing/kayaking—closes the Village in style. Park roads are plowed, closed to motorized vehicles but open to strollers, bikers and rollerbladers. But mostly spring is a time for looking back at fresh powder and looking ahead to leaves and wildflowers. Eventually buds appear on the trees and new green shoots poke up through long brown grasses flattened by months of snowpack.

Summer is coming again!